THE
COLLEGE
ESSAY TRAP

Cassie Nichols

D1235807

CS

COLLEGE SPECIFIC PRESS

Printed in the United States of America. For information, address: College Specific, 1205 De La Vina, Santa Barbara, CA 93101

www.collegespecific.com

The college essay trap: rescue your college application essay from the "maybe" pile / Cassie Nichols / Edited by Daphne Tebbe / 2nd ed.

Book Design by LOTUSCreative / www.lotuscreative.com

ISBN: 978-0-9859118-4-3

Second Edition: May 2015

For Dean Fred, who read my college application essays and gave me a chance anyway.

You must throw up every morning and clean up every afternoon.

— RAY BRADBURY

CONTENTS

INTRODUCTION

Before you start your college application essay, there are two people I would like you to meet.

The first is Jim. Like many admissions officers, Jim is a lifer. He has chosen college admissions as a career. He's worked at three different colleges and universities, each time moving to a more prestigious position. Over the course of his long career, he has developed an ability to open an application folder, read its contents, and swiftly form an idea of who a student really is.

It's not an easy job. Every year, in addition to all his duties, Jim is charged with deciding the fate of outstanding students who have dedicated the last four years of their lives to impressing him at this one, crucial moment. He doesn't take this responsibility lightly.

The second person I want you to meet is Paula. She's an admissions officer too, but of a different sort. Recently graduated, she's not sure if this is the career she wants, or whether it will end up being a stepping-stone to law school or graduate school. But she loves her alma mater, and like Jim, she takes her responsibility seriously.

This is Paula's first year reading applications and essays, but over the years, Jim has evaluated thousands of them. Over the course of their "reading season," they will work through an average of thirty applications every day.

One more minor note about Jim and Paula: they don't actually exist. They are composites of all the college admissions officers I have ever known, talked to, and read about. As director of College Specific, I spend a tremendous amount of time with my students on their college essays. Whenever I review a draft, admissions officers like Jim and Paula are foremost in my mind.

Throughout this book, I'll refer to Jim and Paula as I share several stories of past experiences working with students on their essays. Jim and Paula will serve as our guides, helping us understand the essay from the standpoint of the college admissions officer.

AVOIDING THE "TRAP"

Most bookstores have an entire shelf of books dedicated to the college admissions process, and many deal specifically with the essay. There are books that promise to help you develop the perfect college essay in ten steps, or in eight steps, or even in four steps. Then there are the collections: the essays that will "get you into Harvard," or the 50 "best" college essays in the history of mankind.

There are many, many methods, each promising results. But the truth is that there are no hard-and-fast rules on how to approach what many consider to be the most intimidating— and important—part of the application process. Everyone understands that colleges want a well-written, thoughtful, and personalized story. But how much does that knowledge really help you when you're trying to tell *your* story?

As a student, you will likely spend a lot of time researching, perhaps scribbling in the margins of the aforementioned books, in an effort to understand what you're expected to say in your college essay. When you read those countless "perfect" essays, you'll be tempted to mold yourself into someone else—someone all the experts are telling you to be. This is a trap.

There is no real consensus on what the college essay should include—other than strong, convincing writing. Colleges give you the freedom to take your essay

COLLEGES GIVE YOU THE FREEDOM TO TAKE YOUR ESSAY AND RUN WITH IT.

and run with it. They want you to make it entirely your own.

There *is* a consensus, however, on what admissions officers are hoping *not* to see. There are a number of very common mistakes that students make, time and again, that can easily be avoided. Things that make Jim and Paula, and their real-world counterparts, yearn to move on to the next applicant. Learning what these mistakes are, and how to avoid them, will give you a much fuller understanding of what colleges want—in fact, need—in order to decide whether you'll fit at their school.

That's why I wrote this short book: to help you set yourself apart by avoiding the most common essay pitfalls.

Like most traps, the college essay trap is easy to avoid. You just have to know what to look for.

01 THE ENGLISH TRAP

I remember thinking to myself: this kid's a good writer. I sat there, pen in hand, scanning a strong thesis, orderly topic sentences, and cited quotations. Everything was where it should be. Flawlessly executed. This would be an A paper in any English class I'd ever taught.

But this essay wasn't intended for an English teacher; it was intended for a college admissions officer. And as a college application essay, it didn't pass the test.

Its author, Jacob, was a senior from Wisconsin. Two hours earlier, he had sent me a frantic email after stumbling across the College Specific website. His college applications were due in less than a week, and he wanted to make sure his main essay was on the right track.

He was expecting minor corrections. He had stayed up late for the past few nights, arranging his paragraphs, tweaking every word, and drawing on everything his English teachers had drilled into him over the years. Surely, he thought, this essay would increase his odds of getting into college.

What I had to tell Jacob, in the softest terms possible, was that minor corrections wouldn't cut it. What he had sent me was not a college essay; it was an English paper. In it, he spoke in glowing terms about one of his favorite books as a child, *Robinson Crusoe*. The focus, however, was on Crusoe, not on Jacob. Perhaps more damaging, he had written the quintessential five-paragraph essay, with each body paragraph focusing in great detail on Crusoe. I read through the essay and learned a lot about Crusoe, but very little about Jacob.

TRAP #1: SUBMITTING YOUR ENGLISH PAPER

I read essays like Jacob's all the time, and the tendency to produce an English paper is completely understandable. Throughout your high school career, you've been taught to write a certain way, and you've rarely been allowed to stray from it. Formulas such as these have been drilled into your head:

> *Thesis+topic sentences+evidence+conclusion = good writing*

> *Five paragraphs = ideal essay length*

This knowledge is far from a bad thing. You'll use it in college, where you'll be asked to support your arguments, reference your main points, and remain organized and concise along the way. It will also help you in the real world, when you're asked to write a cover letter for a job application. In a competitive job market, you're better off if you can state why you're an ideal candidate in a front-and-center thesis statement.

But as counter-intuitive as it may seem, formulaic writing is the worst thing you can use when you're trying to get into college. College admissions officers want you to take risks. They want you to tell your own story in your own voice.

Why? Think of Jim, the admissions officer I introduced you to earlier. Try to imagine his life. Jim is knee-deep in the middle of application reading season. He hasn't slept much lately. He has worn the same outfit to work for the past week. His hair is unbrushed, his eyes bloodshot, and his girlfriend is beginning to wonder what happened to him. On one particularly brutal day full of application reviews, he finds himself slumped over his desk. It's 2 a.m., and the rest of campus is peacefully asleep. Jim has been going stir crazy after a long day spent reading dozens of essays, from dozens of applicants, all of whom have amazing grades and stellar résumés brimming with awards and accomplishments.

AN IMPORTANT NOTE ABOUT RISK TAKING: THIS APPLIES TO YOUR WILLINGNESS TO GET PERSONAL, NOT TO YOUR WRITING STYLE.

AVOID COMING OFF AS KOOKY, QUIRKY, OR TRYING TOO HARD. COLLEGES DON'T WANT A FORMAL FIVE-PARAGRAPH ESSAY, BUT THEY DON'T WANT AN ESSAY WRITTEN IN KLINGON, DOTHRAKI, OR IAMBIC PENTAMETER EITHER.

Jim has two applications to go before he can call it a night. He opens one: perfect grades, scores, etc. He then begins to read the essay:

Throughout high school, I could relate to Elizabeth Bennett, Jane Austen's heroine in Pride and Prejudice, in three major ways: our worldview, ability to admit mistakes, and tolerance of others.

Something inside Jim whimpers and dies. *Not another one,* he groans. His eyes glaze over, and he thinks longingly of Fiji as he dutifully plows through the essay and throws the application on the "maybe" pile.

Then, salvation. Jim opens the second application, reading the essay's first two sentences.

I never made a single mistake until I was fourteen years old. It was a heavy burden.

His heart starts beating again. He feels a twinge of excitement; he's going to learn something about the person who wrote this. He's on the verge of actually discovering, through a well-written essay, an applicant's personality and character. And as an admissions officer, that's all he really wants.

Above all else, remember this: the college essay is the only direct bridge between you and the people who decide whether you belong at their school.

The rest—your grades, your extracurricular activities, your test scores, and your recommendation letters—all matter immensely. They convey who you are as a student in high school, and they suggest the kind of student you'll be in college.

But none of these metrics have the ability to convey who you are as a person like the college essay can. Knowing this, why would you choose to hide behind a stuffy, analytical essay?

> THE COLLEGE ESSAY IS THE ONLY DIRECT BRIDGE BETWEEN YOU AND THE PEOPLE WHO DECIDE WHETHER YOU BELONG AT THEIR SCHOOL.

Admissions officers have read *Pride and Prejudice*; they have read *Robinson Crusoe*. They don't want to read these books again. They want to read about you.

Consider the second opening line again, the one that resurrected Jim from his zombie-like stupor:

> *I never made a single mistake until I was fourteen years old. It was a heavy burden.*

You're interested, right? This writer is about to tell a story; not about a fictional character from the 19th century, but about himself. These first couple sentences don't reveal much in the way of context, but that's okay. This writer has used his sense of wit and humor to grab Jim's attention. There's a promise that a personal story is about to unfold. More importantly, there's trust on the part of the writer that Jim will keep reading.

That trust is important; the first writer has zero trust in Jim. In fact, Jim knows exactly what's next: a paragraph comparing the writer's worldview to that of Elizabeth Bennett, another comparing their newfound ability to admit mistakes, then another droning on about their respective abilities to tolerate others. Why on earth should Jim read further? He's already made up his mind. He's got one foot in bed already.

When it comes to the college essay, feel free to break some rules. Many still apply, of course: you need to watch your grammar and spell everything correctly. Sentence structure still matters. But the formula that got you A's in English can be a straitjacket when you're writing your college essay. In this case, however, it's not your arms that are immobilized. It's your voice.

WHEN IT COMES TO THE COLLEGE ESSAY, FEEL FREE TO BREAK SOME RULES.

In an English paper, you're expected to be analytical. You know the drill: "Talk about the significance of the green light in *The Great Gatsby*," or, "What role does colloquial language play in *The Adventures of Huckleberry Finn*?" At this point, you could write one of these essays in your sleep. So the temptation is strong to return to this familiar format in your college essay. But the last thing you want to do is sleepwalk—in a straitjacket—through the college essay. There are too many pitfalls along the way.

One of the biggest pitfalls is the temptation to recycle. Why not just dust off that essay your AP English teacher liked so much? You got an A on it. Surely the folks in the admissions office at Columbia will like it too.

Trust me, they won't. They already assume you've been taught the basics. Also, they're more sophisticated than you may realize. They'll suspect after the first few sentences that you've simply tweaked an old English paper, and they won't be impressed. Worse yet, they might stop reading altogether.

Jacob only had a few days left before his application was due. There wasn't time to rewrite the whole essay, but there was still time to infuse it with his personality.

To figure out how to do that, we had a long chat about Jacob's experience with Robinson Crusoe, both the character and the novel. Luckily, it wasn't just some book he'd been forced to write about in English class. This book actually meant something to him on a personal level. That was our starting point.

We sifted through his essay, pulling out the nuggets that provided insight into his—Jacob's, not Crusoe's—character. Crusoe was a solitary figure; so was Jacob, whose childhood was punctuated by frequent moves. Living in a different town every few years made it difficult for him to cultivate long-term friendships. Yet, like Crusoe, Jacob grew to value relationships and companionship. Jacob had read the book a number of times throughout his childhood, and its meaning had deepened for him over the years.

As he revised his essay, he concentrated on what the book meant to him as a lonely child, the first time he read it. He contrasted those feelings with how the book struck him now, as a young man going off to college. He realized that college, too, is a sort of island, where you discover things every bit as important as what Crusoe found: your intellectual passions, and classmates who will challenge them. He ended up with a deeply moving essay about growing up and learning to embrace relationships with the people around him. He showed a capacity for growth and introspection.

Most importantly, from a college admissions standpoint, this essay was not a five-paragraph essay about Robinson Crusoe. It was a beautifully crafted essay about Jacob.

AVOIDING THE ENGLISH TRAP

How do you avoid the English Trap? First, and perhaps most obviously, write in the first person. Get used to the idea of talking and writing about yourself. One technique I recommend: write your first draft as if you're talking to your best friend. This will help you lay the groundwork.

Second, don't pontificate. Admissions officers don't care how much you know about Robinson Crusoe or Elizabeth Bennett.

They care how much you know about yourself.

Finally, avoid formulas at all costs. Don't let your personality fade into an English teacher's notion of essay structure. Let it shine.

02 THE RÉSUMÉ TRAP

Here's what I learned about Christie: she loved spending time with her small, tight-knit family. She loved their hokey traditions and penchant for long conversations. She loved her high school classes—even the ones that kept her up late. She loved to try new things, even if she knew she wouldn't be good at them. And she loved to make people laugh.

She came to my office near the end of summer, after returning from an annual family road trip. She had just spent weeks in a cramped SUV driving through the western United States with her parents, two younger sisters, and Anna, a foreign exchange student from Spain. High achiever that she was, Christie had spent much of her road trip formulating and writing the perfect college essay.

Christie had actually been excited to write this essay, viewing it as a payoff of sorts. After all, what was the point of all those long hours of hard work and self-discipline throughout high school if not to give her something to brag about in her college essay? Now she could showcase her many achievements.

Here's what her original essay said about her: she was a National Honors Society member; she was the editor in chief of her school paper; she was founder and president of the Chess Club and Recycling Team; she was a Big Sister, cross-country star, and an AP scholar.

It read like the cover letter for a job application. Those compelling personal qualities I'd discovered in my initial meeting with Christie were nowhere to be found, hopelessly lost in a 650-word regurgitation of her college résumé. It was an impressive résumé, but it was an unimpressive college essay. Here's how it opened:

> The last three years of high school have included a ton of activities and experiences. While a few stand out – editing my school newspaper, founding the recycling team and presiding over the chess club, and leading my team to a cross-country league championship, I can honestly say that I don't regret anything I tried. Each and every activity has helped shape me into the person I am today and the person I will continue to be in college.

As I flipped through the folder she had brought with her, I asked Christie: "What is it you want them to learn about you from this essay?" Christie gave me the answer so many college applicants give: "I want them to know that I work hard," she said.

I pulled her transcript from the folder and laid it on the desk in front of her. It was packed with A's in honors and AP classes. Then I pulled out the college résumé she had brought with her, which was nearly five pages long. I reminded her about the evaluations her teachers had been asked to send, which would undoubtedly tout her drive and dedication as a student.

"They already know you work hard," I said. "Your essay is a chance to show them something else about you. Something they can't find in the rest of your application. What *else* do you want them to know?"

TRAP #2: REGURGITATING YOUR RÉSUMÉ

Even if you've never had a job interview, you've seen one on TV: the nervous applicant sits down in front of a huge wooden desk while an intimidating employer scowls, shuffles papers around, then proceeds to ask about the applicant's prior accomplishments. The applicant, trembling with anxiety, gingerly slides his résumé forward and offers a weak smile. It's all perfectly miserable.

Jim the admissions officer may scowl from time to time— you would too if you were forced to stay up late at night and work weekends. He may review your transcript, test scores, recommendation letters, and extracurricular activities as an employer would review a job applicant's résumé and references. Just as an employer would want to know if you can succeed at his company, Jim wants to know whether you have what it takes to succeed at his school.

But the similarity ends there. The job résumé is lifeless. Its purpose is to list and briefly describe a job applicant's professional experience. A college essay, on the other hand, should be full of life. It should be full of nuance and texture. It should tell a story.

Let me give you an example. Here are two different openings. Which do you think will inspire Jim to keep reading?

> *As future ASB President and aspiring AP Scholar, I wondered if I would have the time to serve as editor in chief of The Forge. But I knew I had to try.*

Or:

> *My father's singing voice was an off-key screech that shattered the serene desert silence and sent small animals scurrying for their holes. It's a sound I've grown to love.*

Which essay would you keep reading? One promises to be a mind-numbing list of accomplishments; the other promises to tell a story. Unfortunately for poor Jim, many college applicants don't understand this distinction. They choose the former, jauntily rattling off their achievements and fluffing up some of their more mundane experiences to make them seem more interesting. In the process, they utterly fail to convince Jim that they belong at his college.

Let's switch admissions officers for a moment and give Jim a break. He's not the one reading your essay; Paula is. Remember, Paula is younger and fresh out of college herself. In fact, because Paula is so young, there's a good chance she just graduated from the college to which you are so enthusiastically applying. She's a little less grumpy than Jim, but her expectations are every bit as high. She took this job because she cares about her school.

This is not uncommon. Graduates often take a job in admissions at their alma mater. In fact, more often than not, the person reading your essay will be someone who penned his or her own essay only a few years before. They've had four years to get to know their college, to develop an understanding of the type of student who will thrive in that environment, and the type of student who will not.

Paula loves her school even more than you do. Why else would she choose to stay on campus for another year or two to represent it and, more importantly, to decide who is best equipped to carry on her school's traditions?

Paula and all of her friends had extensive college résumés too. However, their friendship wasn't forged by comparing AP scores or the number of clubs they belonged to in high school. It was about where they came from, what mattered to them, and what they wanted out of life. It was about their character.

This is what Paula is looking for in your college essay: hints about your character. So the goal of your essay, ideally, is to leave Paula with a vague sense of regret that she's too old to be your classmate. Paula won't get to stay up until the wee hours with you, comparing notes about an exciting new school. She won't get to linger over cold food in the dining hall, too engaged in a political debate with you to eat her lasagna while it's hot. She won't get to share a bottomless tub of popcorn with you as you both strive to survive finals.

But if your essay is great—not good, but great—she'll want to. And she'll know that your future classmates will as well.

A college application is not a job interview. So don't treat it as if it were. Your future boss wants to know what experience you are bringing to the company; he wants to get a sense of what kind of person you're going to be when you're on the job.

> A COLLEGE APPLICATION IS NOT A JOB INTERVIEW. SO DON'T TREAT IT AS IF IT WERE.

What you do in the off hours isn't relevant.

Paula, on the other hand, wants to know what kind of person you're going to be when you're on *and* off the job. She knows that students only spend a portion of their time actually attending class and doing homework. She can find out everything she needs to know about your grand accomplishments by looking at the rest of your application: your transcripts, your grades, and your teacher recommendation letters.

But what else will you bring to her school? What are you likely to do on a typical Friday night? Will you represent her school well, on and off campus? What will you bring to campus that will benefit the other students? How will you interact with others? What will really matter to you?

Keep in mind that you're competing with thousands of other applicants, and they have impressive résumés of their own.

At the highly selective colleges in particular, you won't get in simply because you look good on paper.

Paula knows that you have nearly two decades of life experience, that you've overcome challenges and learned important life lessons. She knows that you are unique, and her college has provided a space for you to tell them about it.

Use that space wisely.

Christie used her space very wisely, in the end. She was disappointed, at first, that all the time she'd spent during her road trip had been wasted on an essay that would have to be scrapped. But it was August; she had started early, and she still had a lot of time for rewrites.

Christie and I talked for quite a while before we zeroed in on her topic. We started with her extracurricular activities, discussing everything she had accomplished. But try as we might, we couldn't find a strong enough link between these activities and who Christie was as a person.

This is not unusual; I see this very often with my students, **YOUR EXTRACURRICULAR ACTIVITIES DON'T DEFINE YOU, NOR SHOULD THEY DICTATE YOUR ESSAY TOPIC.** and it's okay. There's more to them than what they do for a few hours after school. So if you're searching for essay topics that pertain to your extracurricular activities and find yourself coming up short, don't panic. Your extracurricular activities don't define you, nor should they dictate your essay topic.

Once we began talking about her family, Christie's demeanor changed completely. The pitch of her voice went up a notch and her gestures became more animated. Having just returned from that annual family road trip, she had plenty to say. I sat there with rapt attention as she launched into one family adventure after another.

To some, long hours in a cramped car would seem unbearable. Christie had sometimes felt the same way, until this summer. This time, instead of endless arguments with her sisters about what music they'd listen to or whose turn it was to sit in the dreaded middle seat, she'd had the opportunity to see the trip through the eyes of someone who'd never taken it before: Anna, their Spanish exchange student.

Early on, Christie had noticed the wonder in Anna's eyes as she saw, for the first time, things that Christie had come to regard as mundane and boring. Anna had laughed out loud at the stone dinosaurs at the rest stop near Palm Springs. She'd been intrigued and delighted by the attractions at Calico Ghost Town. She'd even regarded the scenery during their leg-stretching rest stops with a sense of awe and appreciation.

Growing up in the west, Christie had become accustomed to the vastness of the sprawling desert landscape and the beauty of the sights. Now, she thought about how it might seem to someone to whom all of this was completely foreign. She began to look upon everything with new eyes.

When she looked at her family through these new eyes, she began to realize how special the seemingly ordinary could be: her mother's obsession with fold-out maps, her sisters' tireless replaying of Justin Bieber songs, and her father's off-key singing voice.

So in her essay, instead of raving about her busy high-school life, she highlighted a particularly memorable moment on that family trip: at a roadside rest stop, Christie's father had attempted to teach Anna a song by the Beach Boys, completely oblivious to his own terrible voice and to the horrified glances of passersby.

Later, as the family drove along the open highway, each gazing at a different part of the desert, each lost in private thought, she realized how truly content they all were together—even Anna, who had been a stranger only a few weeks before.

Remember the second opening line from earlier in the chapter?

My father's singing voice was an off-key screech that shattered the serene desert silence and sent small animals scurrying for their holes. It's a sound I've grown to love.

Here, Christie promises humor and introspection, and the rest of her essay delivers on that promise. Through this essay, Paula—or any other admissions officer—would learn that Christie has the ability to step back from everything swirling around her in her busy life and take stock of what matters. This is a valuable skill to have as a busy college student.

AVOIDING THE RÉSUMÉ TRAP

Your college résumé cannot be a substitute for your essay, but it can serve as a good starting point. It can be helpful to see all of your accomplishments and experiences laid out before you, and to select the most meaningful as a foundation for a potential essay topic.

Once you've selected a particular experience, ask yourself what you really want the person who is reading your essay to learn about you. Remember, admissions officers want to understand how you relate to other people and what's important to you.

Now, tell a story. If you choose to write about your tenure as student body president, for example, avoid talking about your campaign strategies or your legislative victories. Instead, dig deep into your memory and think about a moment during this experience when you realized something about yourself. Not the year or the month . . . the moment. That's what you should write about.

Understand: you need to be specific. Draw the reader into that moment with you. Pull them into your world. Show them this tiny slice of yourself. Give them something they would never have known from reading your college résumé.

03 THE PARENT TRAP

Rashi had it easy. At least, she had it easy compared to her parents.

Before Rashi was born, they'd left India to seek new opportunities in the United States. Back then, their day-to-day life hadn't been about family dinners, weekend soccer tournaments, or summer camps. It had been about survival. But they had prospered in America, and Rashi didn't remember much about the hard times.

Still, she had a keen appreciation for everything her parents had given her. She listened to their stories of the "old days" with rapt attention and unbridled admiration. And she also felt a little guilty; she'd been given so much, and she knew she could have worked harder in school while growing up. The previous year, after coming to the realization that she was smarter than her grades suggested, she had begun to turn things around, focusing more on her classes and improving her grades.

When Rashi came to me for help applying to college, I knew she had a great story to tell. We sat for a long time, talking about her childhood, trying to figure out what her essay topic would be. The conversation kept returning to one thing: her parents and their life of sacrifice . . . and the high expectations they'd placed on her. She was expected to excel in school, in sports, and in everything else she did. She understood why the expectations were so high, and she didn't resent it; she knew her parents had given up a lot for her. This knowledge—and the desire to live up to their example—fueled her desire to do better in school.

Knowing how Rashi felt about her parents, I told her to go home and write. No rules, no boundaries. I wanted to see what she would come up with, hoping that she would provide a solid backstory that could serve as a foundation for her actual essay.

A week later, Rashi brought back exactly what I'd hoped for and expected: a three-page essay that recounted, almost exclusively, the hardships her parents had faced, both before and after she'd come into the world.

Her father had put himself through college, then worked his way up the ladder of a company in the paper products industry. He'd worked incredibly long hours and spent a lot of time on the road. Sometimes they hadn't seen him for weeks at a time.

Her mother's story was different. Back in India, she had been an excellent student with lofty ambitions. When she moved to America with Rashi's father, however, circumstances relegated her to a supporting role. She made the decision to give up her dream of studying medicine in India. Instead, as the head of the household, she was the first to wake up every morning, preparing everyone's food and clothing for the day ahead, and she spent many hours at the kitchen table with Rashi, helping her with homework and school projects.

Here's a taste of what Rashi brought to me:

> *Winters were especially hard for my parents. The basement they rented—a basement was all they could afford—was damp, even in summer. In the winter, without heat, it was like a cold, dusty cavern. Every morning, my father would rise before dawn, eat the breakfast my mom had risen even earlier to prepare, and take a bus to his job at the paper factory.*

This wasn't Rashi's story, obviously, but it needed to be written. It needed to be put on paper, a basis for what would become her college essay. Together, we would mine the story of her parents for the nuggets that would illuminate Rashi herself.

Here's the important distinction: what Rashi brought back to me was a great story; it just wasn't *her* story. And, as inspiring as her parents' stories were, they weren't the ones applying to college.

Unfortunately, Rashi's first draft resembled many of the finished essays that admissions officers read. Like Rashi, many students write about their parents' lives and assume that, because the subject of the essay is interesting and compelling, they've done their job. They've shown where they come from, and they assume that's enough.

TRAP #3: TELLING SOMEONE ELSE'S STORY

Imagine if Rashi had submitted this draft as part of her final application. Jim the admissions officer would be impressed with her descriptive powers, and moved by her ability to put herself—and her reader—in her parents' shoes. Rashi hadn't even been born yet, and yet Jim would feel as if she had been in that damp basement with her parents.

Jim would keep reading, waiting to meet Rashi; but because she had spent all of her precious 650 words talking about her parents, he never would. So as much as he would have appreciated Rashi's capable writing, he would have grudgingly slipped her beautiful essay back into her folder, tossing it onto the "maybe" pile with all the other essays that had failed to illuminate their authors.

No matter how well written your essay is, it's not done until it's about you. So whether you're applying using the Common Application or, as Rashi was, applying to a University of California school, you're going to have to show that you

> NO MATTER HOW WELL WRITTEN YOUR ESSAY IS, IT'S NOT DONE UNTIL IT'S ABOUT YOU.

understand how your background helped mold you into the person you are today.

Here are similar prompts from both applications:

> *Describe the world you come from — for example, your family, community or school — and tell us how your world has shaped your dreams and aspirations. (University of California Application)*

> *Some students have a background, identity, interest, or talent that is so meaningful they believe their application would be incomplete without it. If this sounds like you, then please share your story. (Common Application)*

The Common Application's version of the question is less explicit, but they both want the same thing: to know about you. Everything else is just context. Your grandma emigrated from Mexico? Great. Now explain how that has influenced you. Your father lost his job? This was certainly an important event in your life. Your task is to tell us how it shaped you into the person you are now.

Sometimes, finding your own story requires sifting through the larger story around you. In Rashi's case, her parents' history was inexorably intertwined with the young woman she had become. With a little digging, we discovered something that loomed larger than anything else in her childhood, larger even than her father's sacrifice: his absence. He had missed

SOMETIMES, FINDING YOUR OWN STORY REQUIRES SIFTING THROUGH THE LARGER STORY AROUND YOU.

many crucial childhood moments while he was away on business or working late into the night. And yet Rashi knew many of those moments—the recitals, the celebrations, the field trips—would never have occurred if he hadn't been working so hard to make them financially possible.

She realized that her father wasn't the only one who had made sacrifices. He had sacrificed evenings at home and family outings, but she had sacrificed the day-to-day presence of her father. She also knew that she'd never resent him for this: it was their mutual sacrifice that had created all the opportunities she now enjoyed.

There was something else that loomed as large for Rashi as her father's absence: her mother's presence. Since her mother had always been there, day in and day out, for as long as Rashi could remember, Rashi had taken her presence for granted, never really stopping to consider all that her mother had given up to be there for Rashi.

What we learned about Rashi from her final essay was that she was the sort of person who could look beyond her own needs and understand that life—and family relationships—can be complex. Any admissions officer who read Rashi's essay would know exactly what sort of addition she'd be to a college campus. Her ability to see the bigger picture would translate into a willingness to understand the people around her. If she'd focused only on her parents' hardships, no matter how interesting or well-written her essay was, that admissions officer would not know this about her.

This is an integral part of the writing process: **your topic must**

grow. You most certainly have interesting people around you, and it's okay to start with them. But that doesn't mean you're not interesting. Use your parents' story—or your grandma's story, or your brother's story—to punctuate your own.

AVOIDING THE PARENT TRAP

Rashi's process is a good template. If you have interesting stories in your family, try writing them out. When you're done, think about how these have affected you in a personal, tangible way. You might have found a good starting point for your essay.

When you're done with a draft, ask someone else to read it. Hopefully, you have someone whom you trust, but who isn't directly involved. In other words, if the essay involves Grandma, don't give it to Grandpa to read. Give it to a college counselor, or a teacher, or a friend. Ask them if they learned more about Grandma than they did about you. If they feel that they did, you still have work to do.

> DON'T LET YOUR COLLEGE ESSAY READ LIKE A RECOMMENDATION LETTER FOR SOMEONE ELSE.

Don't let your college essay read like a recommendation letter for someone else. As meaningful as the stories of others might be to you, they should only serve as a backdrop for your essay.

04 THE SUPERMAN TRAP

I was eager to meet Aaron. His mom, Karen, came up to me after one of my presentations at a local high school and told me about how they had spent the majority of the summer working on his essay. It was "pretty much done," she told me. Would I have time to give it a quick review?

Uh oh, I thought, with a strong sense of déjà vu.

Karen was like many parents I'd known before: well-educated, well-meaning, and enthusiastic about her child's brilliance and potential. She knew better than most how unique and interesting her son was; she was his biggest cheerleader and cared more than anyone about his future. Who better to guide him through his essay?

When I read Aaron's essay, my fears were confirmed: it read like a Superman comic. Anyone reading it would assume that Aaron could leap tall buildings in a single bound. It was, quite unintentionally, the stuff of fiction:

> *It was dark, cold, and unfamiliar territory, but I trudged ahead anyway. I had arrived before dawn, with a sack lunch in one hand and a hammer in the other. We were there to help. We were there to give people a better life. It was my first vacation in a very long time, and I couldn't think of a better way to spend it than with Habitat for Humanity.*

With Karen's help, Aaron had taken great care to present

himself as flawless, even heroic, as if he had spent his summer building houses with his own two hands.

Here's what Aaron—and Karen—didn't realize: to a college admissions officer, "flawless" can often mean "lifeless." In addition, essays like these often seem insincere, as if the student is trying too hard to be someone he or she isn't.

> TO A COLLEGE ADMISSIONS OFFICER, "FLAWLESS" CAN OFTEN MEAN "LIFELESS."

While Rashi's essay hadn't actually been about her (see Chapter 3), Aaron's essay was about an Aaron who couldn't possibly exist.

TRAP #4: PRETENDING YOU'RE SUPERMAN

Remember our beleaguered admissions officer, Jim? Put yourself in his chair again. Imagine he works at Harvard . . . or Yale or Stanford or Princeton. He has spent months reading essays from superbly capable over-achievers—like Aaron— trumpeting the accomplishments they've amassed during their storied high school careers.

It's not just that Jim is bored (which he most assuredly is), it's also that he cares about his school, and he doesn't want it filled with people who think they've never made mistakes— or who aren't willing to be open about them.

In other words, it's one thing to have a school full of perfect students; it's quite another to have a school full of students who *think* they're perfect.

How refreshing it would be for Jim to stumble upon an essay by a highly capable, obviously brilliant young student who is humble, and who expects to grow and to learn in college.

> IT'S ONE THING TO HAVE A SCHOOL FULL OF PERFECT STUDENTS; IT'S QUITE ANOTHER TO HAVE A SCHOOL FULL OF STUDENTS WHO *THINK* THEY'RE PERFECT.

This is good news for everyone, not just you high achievers: it's okay not to be perfect. You *can* admit mistakes, and you *can* talk about your shortcomings—as long as you show how you deal with them. That's what colleges care about. They know you'll make mistakes in college; they want to know how you'll handle those mistakes.

Often, it can be incredibly powerful to use your essay to show what you do when you're not succeeding. How do you handle disappointment, failure, or confusion? Have you ever taken a risk in school and failed? What has been your greatest regret in high school? How have you changed since then? This is the sort of essay that will tell an admissions officer what he really wants to know: whether he can rely on you to grow in a positive way once you're on his campus.

Here's another way to look at it: as a numbers game. The top colleges, with their record number of applicants and notoriously low acceptance rates, have the luxury of turning away the best of the best, primarily because of their finite number of available slots.

Now, assume you have a handful of "perfect" students—

super high-achieving valedictorian types—in any given high school. At their school, they're special; they represent a tiny percentage of the student body. But there are thousands of high schools in the United States alone, each with high-achieving students applying to the top colleges. Add this to the countless legions of outstanding international applicants, and you will begin to get a sense of how stiff the competition is, even among the so-called "cream of the crop."

How can Aaron—or you—possibly stand out in this pool of "perfect" applicants? By being human.

My biggest task with Aaron was convincing his mother Karen that he needed to start over. They had worked extremely hard on his essay, so this wasn't an easy sell.

We battled—in a friendly way—for almost two weeks. I told her that students don't need to be perfect, and that sometimes admitting weakness can be the most attractive thing to an admissions officer at this level. Perfection is not attractive. It's not even possible, and admissions officers know that.

But Karen was well aware of the field of applicants Aaron was up against. She didn't trust that his character would be enough to sway an admissions officer who was deciding between such accomplished students. I got an earful of information about the competition within his high school alone.

Ultimately, I convinced her of how valuable an objective third party could be. Since I didn't know Aaron, I would be more comparable to the admissions officer who would also be encountering him for the first time. Moreover, as someone who had never met her son, I might be attracted to something she would overlook.

Karen agreed to stand back and let the two of us have a crack at the essay without her. It must have been difficult, but to her credit, she held to it.

When I finally sat down with Aaron, I realized immediately that Karen was right about one thing: any college in the world would be lucky to have this kid on its campus.

I asked him about his essay, and about his experience with Habitat for Humanity. In a congenial, self-deprecating way, he joked with me about how terrible he had been at construction. When he showed up on the first day, it was under the assumption that he would sweep in and master all the necessary skills within a day or two. He laughed at this notion now. He'd had no idea how difficult it would be.

He had an endearing sense of humility, and was quick to laugh at his own flaws. He recounted how his skills were famous among the other Habitaters—not his construction skills, but his sandwich-making skills. He could make a mean ham and cheese.

It was an offhand comment, but I was hooked. He continued, telling me how he had agreed to help with the three-week project in spite of having zero construction experience. He'd tried getting to know the other volunteers. Some had been doing construction for many years, and others, like him, were relatively new. But they all possessed something he didn't: the ability to use a hammer.

The others were kind, but as the first week wore on, he had trouble connecting with them. He willingly performed menial tasks to help the work progress, but he felt unfulfilled, unsure of his value to the team. So he cast about for other ways to help.

One day, he made and brought a bag full of deli sandwiches to the jobsite, and they were an instant hit. He quickly became known among the other workers as "Sammie," and the ice was broken. He bonded with them, creating long-term friendships and appreciating his part, however small, in helping people in dire need of housing. Eventually, he even learned how to use a hammer.

In his new essay, Aaron talked about how it felt to be unnecessary, to lack a purpose, and how, for the first time in his life, he had had to work hard to feel valued. In showing how he had eagerly embraced a supporting role for the good of the project, that endearing humility I had noticed immediately was front and center.

This is the Aaron I wanted the colleges to see: he was brilliant and accomplished, but there was more to him than that. This kid was special precisely because of his imperfections. He was shy—in a disarming way—utterly kind, and highly motivated. He was just the sort of person—academics aside— that colleges are looking for. If he had submitted his original essay, they would never have known that.

His new opening lines hinted at an essay that would reveal who he really was:

> *Among the rest of the crew, my ability to swing a hammer was legendary. So was my inability to hit a nail.*

AVOIDING THE SUPERMAN TRAP

For those of you who, like Aaron, have a lot to brag about on paper, your challenge is a bit different from that of other applicants. You have to push all your accomplishments to the side and make the person reading your essay understand that you see yourself as human.

When I meet with my students, particularly those with high levels of achievement, I try to shift the focus from what they've accomplished to how they've grown as people: as friends, as family members, as students, and as members of their community. Most of the time, this growth can be conveyed with an emphasis on humility: by demonstrating an ability to admit mistakes, a capacity to confront one's own weaknesses, and an understanding—even an expectation— that these will result in future growth.

When you're reviewing your essay, imagine that it's about someone other than you. Someone you don't know too well. Would you like this person? Do you feel like you've learned anything valuable about his or her character? If the answer to either of these questions is anything other than a res‹ "yes," you need to start over.

Admitting a mistake isn't the same as admitting a character flaw. Chances are, your high school experience has been full of important ups and downs. Your college experience will be too. Use your essay to show you're prepared for that.

There's another side to that coin, however: this should not be considered a "strategy," per se. Here's what a former Yale admissions officer told me on the subject: "Discussion of a mistake, a weakness or a shortcoming is a delicate task. Like any other aspect of the essay, it cannot come off as disingenuous."

Aaron used his ineptitude with a hammer as a way to frame his aptitude for teamwork. If you don't have a truly broadening moment where a weakness or mistake helped you understand yourself, don't force it. Don't pretend to be someone you're not.

NOTE TO PARENTS

I understand the temptation to help; that's what parents do. But as counterintuitive as it might seem, the best thing you can do is remove yourself from the essay-writing process.

Understand: admissions officers don't know your child at all. They're learning about him for the very first time. You, on the

.ıer hand, know every detail of your child's life and history. So it is likely that you will make assumptions that won't translate well in your child's essay.

But here's the biggest reason to remove yourself from the process: parents have a strong (and quite understandable) tendency to portray their child through their own eyes. They love their child, they see their child's potential, and they want everyone else to see it too. So even for parents who understand the essay writing process, it can be extremely difficult to present a realistic picture of their child.

05 THE JOCK TRAP

Even though I'd never met him in person, I recognized
Eric's name from the sports section of the local newspaper.
I also knew a bit of his history. He came from a long line of
competitive swimmers who had graced the pool of the local
high school over the years.

He held the door for his mother, introducing them both
before she could say a word. As they settled into my office, I
recognized a familiar smell: chlorine.

It brought back memories from my own days as a swimmer:
hours in the pool, endless laps and drills, and constant
hunger. I pushed a tub of Red Vines toward Eric.

When you think of a jock, certain images arise. Eric embodied
the best of these. Aside from his obvious level of confidence,
he exhibited intense determination—a common trait among
dedicated athletes. I knew from my own experience that
being an athlete requires a willingness to invest an enormous
amount of time and energy to attain a tiny degree of
improvement.

As I watched Eric scarf down my Red Vines and we discussed
his high school experience, it became clear what he would
want to write about. I asked him anyway.

"I was thinking of writing about last year's season," he answered. "I dislocated my shoulder and had to work my way back to full strength." He went on to describe the difficulty he'd endured, both mentally and physically, as he came back from an injury, and the valuable lesson he'd learned in perseverance.

I could tell this had been a pivotal experience for Eric. He wanted colleges to understand the willpower it had taken for him to become the athlete he was.

Unfortunately, he was about to fall into the same trap most student athletes do when they contemplate their college essay: writing about the "big game" or the "moment of truth" or, in Eric's case, "overcoming the injury." I could imagine Jim wincing. There are only so many variations of these stories, and admissions officers have read a thousand incarnations of each.

Picture Jim reading the following paragraph:

> The doctors said I might not be able to swim next season. In a fleeting moment, I saw my dreams of a CIF championship come crashing down around me. I felt like I'd lost someone I loved. Then I told the doctor: "I don't care what anyone says, nobody's going to take my dream away from me."

Now, picture Jim reading the above paragraph again. And again, and again . . . year in and year out.

As a former student athlete, I get it. Whether you're a top recruit, or you're vying for the last spot on the team, your sport is your life. Your teammates are your extended family. Your best athletic performance or your high school's team record are reflections of who you are as a person and what you can achieve if you set your mind to it. It's natural to gravitate toward these strengths when you're writing your college essay.

But please, be careful. The decision to write about your sport should be made with caution. Be mindful of the fact that the rest of your application will be full of references to your athletic career. The essay is an opportunity to offset that, and to prove to Jim and Paula that you're more than just a jock.

TRAP #5: HIDING BEHIND YOUR SPORT

Whether you're in danger of falling into the Jock Trap will depend largely on your recruitment status: that is, if you're highly sought after by college coaches, if you're planning to use your athletic abilities to help you get into a top-ranked academic university, or if you just love sports and want the opportunity to play them as a part of your college experience.

Let's break this down into more detail.

1. TOP RECRUITS

If you're a top recruit, with scholarship offers at Division I programs, I'll be honest: chances are your college essay will probably be of secondary importance. Okay, tertiary. My younger sister, an All-American water polo player, signed early with a nationally-ranked college team and didn't even write her essay until her acceptance had been guaranteed. Her admission had nothing to do with her college essay. In fact, many universities with top athletic programs don't even include a college essay requirement as part of their application. For those that do, the more straightforward and non-controversial your essay, the better.

2. ASPIRING IVY LEAGUE OR TOP LIBERAL ARTS ATHLETES

For recruited athletes hoping for a spot at an Ivy League university or a top-ranked liberal arts college, academic expectations are high. You'll be expected to produce stellar grades and test scores, along with evidence of athletic talent and leadership in the rest of your application.

Keep in mind, Jim may or may not have been a jock. You can't count on him to understand or properly appreciate your long hours of practice or early morning workouts.

Furthermore, Jim has sifted through your college résumé, and he already knows about your championship season. He already knows you were elected team captain this year. By extension, he understands the degree to which you've dedicated yourself to your sport. Perhaps there's even a note in your application file from the college coach, who has put in a good word for you.

But none of this matters unless Jim can be convinced that you're grounded and humble—that despite your many athletic successes, you'll bring more to his campus than just your athletic talent.

Consider, for example, a four-year varsity soccer player, also the team's leading scorer and recently-elected senior captain. She would like to write her essay about her commitment to club soccer and how she sacrificed countless weekends and summer vacations for her sport.

But what if her essay had nothing to do with soccer? What if, like most athletes, she had dedicated herself to other pastimes as well? Perhaps she was also a volunteer in the maternity ward of the local hospital, and instead chose to write about the first time she held a newborn baby. She could share how she felt as she gazed down at the brand new life she held in her arms. Reading this, Jim would discover a layer to this obviously capable athlete that he otherwise would not have appreciated: evidence of passion and depth that would provide him with a more complete and compelling picture of her as a person.

3. NON-RECRUITS AND CASUAL ATHLETES

For athletes who haven't been recruited, or for whom playing a sport in college is a secondary consideration, writing about a sport can actually be a positive contribution to the application, demonstrating balance and an ability to excel across a wide range of interests.

A former Yale admissions officer had this to say on the subject:

> *Writing about one's sports experience can be effective in certain circumstances. It could be refreshing to read an essay from a kid who is captain of his or her sports team, but who is also very bright in the classroom and perhaps also editor of the school paper, a member of the debate team, etc. An essay about sports and team leadership from a kid who has perfect grades makes us see him or her as more well-rounded; in other words, not ultra-focused on academic perfection. In other instances, kids might write about sports as an outlet for what is a highly stressful high school environment. It can be reassuring to see this as an admissions officer—they know how to blow off steam, and it's likely they can do this through intramural or club sports at college.*

In other words, whatever you write about in your essay should complete the picture of who you are—without being redundant. If you're a math whiz whose application boasts national awards and top math honors, you don't need to convince Jim of your mathematical prowess. So writing about your love of basketball would be refreshing.

It always matters to me *why* students want to talk about certain things, even if the topic itself isn't going to work. Often, the core of what they are trying to convey is valuable and illuminating.

As Eric told me about his shoulder injury, I began to realize what it was about this particular instance, and physical health in general, that was important to him. More importantly, I learned how much Eric valued his family, and why.

One thing I didn't mention earlier: when Eric came in for our initial meeting and held the door open for his mother, it was because she was in a wheelchair. He then helped situate her and made sure the area we chose could accommodate her. All of the qualities I mentioned earlier—his determination, his confidence, and his steadfastness—were obvious to me within the first few minutes . . . and we were nowhere near a pool.

As we talked, I learned that a car accident years before had left his mother unable to walk. Speaking to him, it was apparent that this was a large part of his intrinsic sense of humility: he realized how vulnerable humans can be. It deeply affected how he approached everything, from athletics to family life.

I came to learn a lot about Eric's family. Eric's mother never missed his swim meets, and neither did his little sister. Eric never missed his sister's ballet recitals or their family potlucks. And one tiny ritual stood out: every Sunday, Eric and his mom attended the local farmers market to buy fresh vegetables for the coming week. It had been a game for them since he was very young, seeing who could find the best bell pepper or orange. While this might seem mundane—or, in Eric's words, "lame"—I could tell it was important to them because it was a tradition that predated his mother's accident. They used to walk through the market together, holding hands. Now, he pushed her.

Eric's college essay focused on the difference between then and now: on the tragedy of his mother's accident, and the unexpected emotional growth that had resulted from it. The accident and its aftermath had drawn the family closer together. Where many young men feel invincible, the accident had instilled in Eric a deepened understanding of human frailty. Those Sundays at the farmers market illustrated this more meaningfully than any run-of-the-mill story about overcoming a sports injury.

In the end, Eric's essay was profoundly moving, highlighting all the personal qualities that contributed to his success as an athlete . . . without mentioning his sport once.

AVOIDING THE JOCK TRAP

If you're eager to share your love for your sport in your essay, ask yourself why this is the case. Perhaps it is because sports often bring out the best in us: the ability to handle challenges, including losing, to balance all the expectations and the pressures we face, and to communicate effectively with others. For many students, sports can be a microcosm of the ssons in life that are most worth learning.

The problem, of course, is that these lessons are shared by many students, and consequently become the topic of many, many college essays. It's a trap to assume that the lessons you've learned as an athlete are unique.

Try using a different approach. Ask yourself what, specifically, you would like to convey through your "sports" essay. Then ask yourself whether, as in Eric's case, you can communicate this through another topic.

If you do decide to write about your sport, there is a cliché blacklist. Do not, under any circumstances, subject Jim to the following, or any variation thereof:

I sacrificed my social life for my sport.

Everything I learned about life, I learned on the court.

I discovered the meaning of life when I was benched for a week and forced to sit on the sidelines.

Everything culminated in that last-second, game-winning shot—the hundreds of hours, gallons of sweat, mind-numbing pain—all for the love of the game.

Steer clear of the above, keep it genuine, and write about something that is meaningful to you. Take your time choosing a topic. It will be tempting to go with the most obvious one, especially for you athletes. But keep in mind that the easiest topics will also be the ones most commonly chosen.

As an athlete, you've spent your life trying to set yourself apart on the court or on the field. Approach your essay in the same way.

06 THE MINOR TRAPS

I've pointed out the worst of the college essay traps, and told you how to get around them. You've learned how to spark Jim and Paula's interest; more to the point, you've learned how to avoid inviting their rejection.

However, there are a few more traps I'd like to mention—comparatively minor, but still noteworthy. While these aren't necessarily as egregious as the ones I've talked about up to this point, they're every bit as common and will still make Jim and Paula pull their hair out in clumps.

Watch out for the following:

THE HAWTHORNE TRAP

> *Throughout the vainglory of my early years and lasting well into the restless torpidity of adolescence, it was made manifestly conspicuous to me by an unfaltering conflux of affirming events that I lacked the wherewithal, so common among my puerile counterparts, to effectuate a single, solitary error.*

Did you stop reading at the word "vainglory"? So did Jim. To him, there's nothing impressive about an ability to consult a thesaurus. Few writers can get away with the flowery linguistic contortions that novelists like Nathaniel Hawthorne are famous for. As the above example shows, no college application essayist should try.

Don't get me wrong: I love Hawthorne as much as the next English teacher. But in a college essay, you're trying to humanize all the test scores, grades, and other data that make up the rest of your application. Lofty language will have precisely the opposite effect. It will distance you from the reader.

WHEN IT COMES TO THE ESSAY, LESS IS MORE.

When it comes to the essay, less is more. Remember, you're trying to convey that you're an interesting, thoughtful, and intelligent person. Moreover, you're generally expected to do it in 650 words.

Compare the long-winded example I just gave to the sample sentence we saw in Chapter One:

> *I never made a single mistake until I was fourteen years old. It was a heavy burden.*

Notice that exactly the same sentiment is conveyed, but without the grandiloquent fluff. This time, you've saved space, conveyed a sense of wit, and hooked the reader.

Don't try to impress them with loaded language. Trust your own voice.

> *The reasons that I have for wishing to go to Harvard are several. I feel that Harvard can give me a better background and a better liberal education than any other university. I have always wanted to go there, as I have felt that it is not just another college, but is a university with something definite to offer. Then too, I would like to go to the* **same college as my father.** *To be a "Harvard man" is an enviable distinction, and one that I sincerely hope I shall attain. - John Fitzgerald Kennedy, 1935*

When our former president applied to Harvard in 1935, his family connections meant there was little doubt that he would be accepted and attend. Believe it or not, the above essay—reprinted here in its entirety—was acceptable back then. It's hard to imagine it would be today.

You may think you're destined for a particular school—USC, for example, because Grandpa dressed you up as a Trojan for your first Halloween—but you still have to convince the USC admissions officers that you're qualified to be there.

Don't waste your precious essay space detailing how and why your father, older sister, or grandfather attended their illustrious institution. Yes, it increases your chances of admission if you come from a long line of USC graduates, but USC will have figured out your "legacy" status from the rest of your application. What matters more to them is whether you fit, and that's what this essay is for.

Assume they care who you are, not what your last name happens to be.

THE OP-ED TRAP

> *I don't understand how anybody could have voted for our state governor; either for what he represents, or for the man he has shown himself to be. When I get to college, I intend to major in political science, increase my political awareness, and find others to stand by my side and fight to protect our country.*

You may have strong feelings about politics, religion, or culture, and that's fine. But be respectful. Understand that the people reading your essay have opinions of their own. They don't mind if you don't agree with them; in fact, they are actively seeking a student body with a diverse set of opinions. Why? Because they feel that a variety of perspectives will foster a healthy learning environment and promote critical thinking skills.

What will turn them off, however, is an essay that is disrespectful of divergent opinions, or that shows an unwillingness to consider all sides of an argument. Remember: as they read your essay, they're going to picture you interacting with other students and teachers, and they want to know that you'll engage in constructive dialogue with those around you. Show them you're capable of this.

If you feel strongly about a potentially divisive topic, be thoughtful. And remember, your essay still needs to be a story about you. It can't read like an op-ed column.

No political tirades allowed.

THE COMEDY TRAP

> *Dear Mr. Admissions officer. I know what you're thinking: wow, this kid's incredible! How can I convince him to come to my school? But wait, there's more! I still have a whole essay left to impress you with, and I plan on using it to my advantage. So sit back, relax, and enjoy the ride!*

Congratulations. Jim just quit his job, and it's your fault.

Humor is a wonderful thing. And it's okay—in fact, it's great—if you can make Jim and Paula laugh. But when you're writing a college essay, and you try to be funny, you have a few things working against you.

First, you don't know the people reading your essay. Humor can be subjective, and the things that make your friends and family laugh might be lost on a reader who has never met you. An admissions officer might find your humor silly—or worse yet, offensive.

Second, keep in mind that you're dealing with text. A joke that works in person might not translate well onto paper.

If you have a natural wit, chances are it will show in your writing. But don't force it. You want your other personality traits—kindness, thoughtfulness, and curiosity—to shine through as well. Don't let a forced attempt at humor overshadow them.

This doesn't rank high on the list of traps. But it happens a lot, and it's easy to avoid.

THE COLUMBUS TRAP

> *Last summer I accompanied my family to China, and it forever changed the way I view myself. For four weeks we trekked across the country, and each day a new adventure unfolded. As I wandered through the crowded streets of Shanghai, the busy markets of Kunming, and the rural countryside of Sichuan, I constantly found myself realizing just how fortunate I was . . .*

Traveling abroad can be a life-altering experience. It can broaden your horizons and trigger profound realizations about the world and your place in it. There's nothing wrong with having this sort of epiphany.

However, there's nothing uncommon about it either. Admissions officers slog through hundreds of these travelogues every season. Jim has a tall, teetering pile of "summer abroad" essays. Not too long ago, Paula had her own summer abroad experience. She, too, had daily epiphanies, so she's not likely to be impressed by the fact that you built huts in Guatemala, studied Mandarin in rural China, or backpacked through the Swiss Alps.

It's not that you can't write about your travels: you can. But stay away from the formulaic canard where, after seeing the world for the first time, you gained a new sense of gratitude for what you have and where you come from. It's just too commonplace.

Instead, focus on a moment in your journey that had special meaning for you. Perhaps there was a particularly rewarding interaction with a local. Or a moment of frustration or anxiety. Search for something specific that will show the reader who you are.

Because—as I've said many times by now—this essay is about *you*. Everything else is window dressing.

EPILOGUE

A FINAL WORD ON THE COLLEGE ESSAY TRAP

There is, of course, one final trap. And it's the biggest one, the granddaddy of all traps. It's also the one that is easiest to fall into, regardless of your scholastic aptitude or writing skills.

The biggest essay trap is failing to take the essay seriously in the first place. In Chapter One, I talk about the English Trap, and how the college essay is not an English paper. That comparison applies in another way as well: it's not something you can write the night before it's due, receive a grade a few weeks later, and never think about again. It's something that takes time, consideration, and a lot of writing.

Authors do multiple rewrites before they submit their manuscript to a publisher. Musicians spend many hours refining their performance before they step onto a stage. As odd as this might seem, you need to think of your college essay in those terms. You need to treat it as a work of art. A creation.

So take it seriously. Start with an idea, start early, and pace yourself. Understand that it will take several drafts to produce a strong college essay. And understand that it's okay if, at some point, you realize your topic is weak and you have to start over (for help with topics and prompts, drop by the College Specific website at http://collegespecific.com).

Also, it's hard to overstate the importance of storytelling in your essay. Make your readers feel like they're there with you, experiencing what you experienced. Make them feel like they know you and understand what matters to you. It's much easier to do this through a story.

At the beginning of this book, I quote the late author Ray Bradbury, famous for his imagination and ability to inspire both readers and writers. When asked about the writing process, he responded:

> *You must throw up every morning and clean up every afternoon.*

For years, I've recited this quotation to my students as they begin the essay-writing process. At first, they are mystified, but they soon realize that the advice it conveys is crucial. Bradbury understood that the least pleasant—and often messiest—part of writing is the beginning: the first draft.

Take Bradbury's advice. If you approach your essay with the understanding that your early drafts are likely to feel scattered and disjointed, you will find that taking that initial plunge isn't so hard. Throw up now, knowing that you will clean up later.

Likewise, one of the worst things you can do is decide you're finished when you're not. Plan on spending months working on your essay, not days. Expect the frequent realization that your essay needs yet another round of editing. **When you think you're done, chances are you're not. Keep going.**

Throw up, clean up, and repeat as necessary.

ACKNOWLEDGMENTS

I first taught the college essay to high school seniors in an educational environment that expected the best from both its students and its teachers. As an English teacher at Choate Rosemary Hall, I was given the freedom to design and implement my own curriculum, and that's exactly what I did during the first two weeks of school, when my seniors were tasked with writing their college essays.

As I taught the essay for the first time, I had a tremendous amount of support from my colleagues at Choate, particularly Chip Lowery, Raman Menon, and Doug James, whose generous guidance on college essay writing was indispensible. I also had Jessica Johnson at my side, mentoring me with kindness and patience during a chaotic and exciting first term, as well as Dean Easton, my officemate and unofficial therapist. Finally, I could always count on Cyrus Cook, my fearless department head, to treat me as though I were a veteran with something important to add to every conversation. With my colleagues' support, I fell in love with teaching and developed a deep affection for the college essay.

Later, I applied to a single graduate school, determined to work with Dr. Sheridan Blau, renowned scholar in the teaching of literature and writing, then a professor at UCSB and now at Columbia's Teachers College. For a year and a half, I absorbed Sheridan's dedication to curriculum development, both through his literary contributions and his classroom teaching methods. Sheridan's students know how much he relies on telling stories and personalizing his lessons, and how effective this approach can be.

As an educator, my greatest reward comes from the meaningful experiences I have with my students. Every year they amaze me, both in their writing and in our conversations, all of which have helped me visualize the sort of book I wanted to write.

Most importantly, I'm grateful to my family and friends, who have helped me stay motivated, confident, and passionate throughout this process. I thank them for putting up with me.

Extra special thanks, for various reasons, to: Tod Lancaster, Derrick Jong, Nicholas Strohl, Daphne Tebbe, James Nichols, Consuelo Benavidez, Miranda and Pablo Nichols, Savannah Lancaster, Daria Etezadi, Jess Davis, Judi Koper, Steve Antonoff, Shannon Brady, Jeremy Vaa, San Marcos High School's AVID students, Lisa McLaughlin, Ellen Gaddie, Blair Dean, Brian Chuckie Roth, Mark Walsh, my Choate students, my Orange County families, and my Santa Barbara families.

Made in the USA
San Bernardino, CA
30 April 2015